The Psalms, Distilled in Verse

by

Jan Christophersen

The Psalms, Distilled in Verse

Jan Christophersen

ISBN: 978-0-9744551-0-5

Cover Design by Chris Mackey, AURA Design Group

The Psalms, Distilled in Verse

Introduction

Every word or phrase contains within it a whole world.

When reading scripture aloud and at the same time listening beyond the words, rise and fall in the listener's imagination. These multi-layered images awaken, delight, challenge, and inspire the focused listener.

Sometimes the pictures and ideas created by a flow of words can slip by us. They can be so many and varied that they flow through our consciousness too quickly to grasp, much less savor. For centuries contemplative teachers have shown Christian readers how to move over scripture's words and phrases, pausing occasionally to let themselves sink into the words.

Within scripture, the Psalms have long been used for prayer. Their wonderful images and varied emotions offer a ready resource for anyone struggling to find words. Yet even the Psalms can take too many words. It is such times that Jan Christophersen's psalm-poems may come to our aid. Jan has read each psalm, listened to its images and layers, savored its meanings, and distilled it into carefully. She offers us her prayerful discernment of each psalm's heart, expressed with sensitivity and respect.

Set aside busyness. Put away the "to-do" list. Turn off the TV and telephone. Sit quietly, read slowly, and let the worlds behind the words of Jan's poems speak to you and for you.

Catherine R. Powell, M Div.

Wilmington, North Carolina

Preface

The emotions of the psalms range from sublime adoration of God to desire for terrifying revenge on enemies. Because they express so many feelings, they can be used as prayer when a person has trouble finding appropriate words.

I have studied each individual psalm and distilled it in my own words in poetry. In some of the verses I have tried to capture the feeling of the whole psalm in a shortened form; in others, I have used a familiar line. These poems can stand on their own, or they can be read alongside the corresponding psalm in the Bible.

I hope you'll find my verses useful adjuncts to your prayer and worship.

Most of these poems were written during silent retreat times at The Pelican House, a building overlooking the ocean at Trinity Camp and Conference Center. My dear friend Lisa Richey is the spiritual director for these retreats. A few years ago a special friend came into my life, Lucia Robinson, who has given editorial advice for my poems. I am so very grateful for these friends, my priest The Reverend Catherine Powell, and my fellow pilgrims on our faith journey at Church of the Servant, Episcopal.

Jan Christophersen

Wilmington, North Carolina

Psalm 1

Blessed are we people

who delight in God's law,

for God's law is to love

and to worship in awe.

As fruit trees prosper

by streams of water,

our lives grow deep roots

from God's wellspring of love,

and we blossom and flourish,

giving plentiful fruit.

Psalm 2

Kings on their thrones

and rulers of men

think they are gods,

and God laughs at them.

Lest God be angry,

remember who reigns.

Blessed are they

who take refuge in him.

Psalm 3

Deliver me, oh God,

from fears without, within,

surrounding me

like enemies.

Watch over me at night.

Banish terror, dreams and fright.

Then--blessed, refreshed--

I'll awaken with delight.

Psalm 4

Hear my prayer, oh God.

Answer me when I call.

I bring you my anger and shame.

Trusting, I give you my all.

You give me space for dark thoughts;

then I listen and wait.

You give me joy in my heart,

and only in you am I safe.

Psalm 5

In the morning I wake and I pray:

prepare for me a straight way.

I'm rejoicing and singing today.

Bless me, oh God, this new day.

Psalm 6

Comfort me in your love.

I've flooded my bed with my tears.

I'm troubled down to my bones.

Save me from sorrows and fears.

Psalm 7

Some people are pregnant with evil,

birthing violence and lies in the world,

but they fall in the holes they have dug,

and their evil returns on their heads.

Judge me, oh God, for my deeds.

I repent of the wrong I have done.

Returning to you, I give thanks,

for in you are my safety and home.

Psalm 8

Holy, holy is your name,

creator of all that came to be--

heaven and earth and moon and stars--

and yet you care for me.

Honor and power you give to us,

to take care of the fish in the sea,

the birds and the beasts and all that live.

Praise to you for your majesty.

Psalm 9

You forget not the poor in the world
whose only hope is in you.
You shelter the needy and weak
as you judge what the rich nations do.

Psalm 10

Where are you, oh God,

when evil seems to reign?

When no one good opposes those

who kill and seize and maim?

The fatherless cry out for you.

You hear their anguished calls.

Justice now is in your hands

as you bring peace to all.

Psalm 11

Evil tries to strike

at fundamentals

of trust and justice.

But all its efforts

are inconsequential,

for God is supreme

and watches us all.

She will redeem.

Psalm 12

Double-crossing people

with lies within their mouths

seem to rule the world.

On every side they prowl.

Help us now, oh God.

You alone are pure and true.

Guard us and protect us.

Our safety is in you.

Psalm 13

Do not forget me, oh God.

How long a time must I wait

and carry this sorrow and pain?

Dark are the nights and the days.

But still I will trust in your love.

You bless me in myriad ways.

I will sing to you and rejoice,

for you hear me, oh God, when I pray.

Psalm 14

"There is no God,"

    a fool would say.

A fool would say

    that man alone

    can rule the day.

Psalm 15

Who is holy in your sight?

Who lives by rules for what is right?

Those who are compassionate,

who do not take advantage

of the innocent, and the advocate

who stands against the reprobate.

Psalm 16

You are my safety and refuge.

You are my joy and delight.

You are my teacher and guide,

my strength in the day and the night.

You show me the path of my life.

In you I rejoice and am glad.

My cup is full of your love.

My soul is secure in your hand.

Psalm 17

Protect me, oh God, from bad ways.

I have followed the law in all things.

Keep me forever in your sight

and under the shadow of your wings.

Psalm 18

Who makes the earth reel and roll?

Who sends the lightning and cold,

hailstones and rainstorms and light,

dark clouds and sunshine so bright?

The Lord does: my refuge, my rock,

my Savior, my strength and my God.

In distress, I implore him to hear.

He saves me from all that I fear.

Psalm 19

The heavens are telling the glory of God.

The stars and the sun are a hymn without words.

The beauty of nature shows God's perfect work.

The voice of creation is heard on the earth.

Psalm 20

In trouble we call you.

We offer our shame.

You answer our pleadings.

Praised be your name!

God is the answer,

my true heart's desire.

She fulfills my soul's promise.

In God is my life.

Psalm 21

My soul's true desire
is abundance of life.
You fulfill all my longings
with blessings divine.

Psalm 22

Oh God, I am sick,

sick at heart, sick in mind.

You've left me forsaken.

You've left me behind.

I'm taunted and troubled.

My thoughts are like beasts,

snarling hatred and anger.

Wild thoughts never cease.

And yet, I remember,

as a babe I was safe,

protected and loved

at my mother's soft breast.

I beg you to help me.

My strength is all gone.

Now only in you

am I safe, am I strong.

Psalm 23

The Lord is my shepherd,

and I am his sheep.

He always protects me.

In comfort I sleep.

With goodness and mercy

my cup overflows.

I follow my shepherd

wherever he goes.

Psalm 23, alternate

You prepare a table before me

in the presence of my enemies

of fear and rejection, lies and deception.

You prepare a place for me

when I've never felt wanted, never belonged.

You nourish my soul.

You feed me rich foods

of acceptance and value and worth.

You honor my deepest longings.

My cup's running over

with unconditional love.

I'm forgiven and whole.

Psalm 24

The earth is the Lord's,

and all its creation.

Who shall ascend

to God's holy nation?

Those with pure hearts.

Those who are pardoned.

Hear what God says:

Lift up your heads!

He stands at your doorway,

radiant in glory.

Let him come in

to transform you within.

Psalm 25

I lift up my soul,

and I am lifted up,

forgiven and blessed

by the God whom I trust.

I follow God's path,

his pathway of love.

It teaches me truth

from the God whom I trust.

Psalm 26

I love to be in your house,

to be where your company dwells.

I try to be honest and true.

Keep me close, and all will be well.

Psalm 27

God is my Savior and light,

the face that I turn to in need.

I am never afraid and forsaken

when God is the one whom I seek.

Psalm 28

When I pray and no answer comes,

and it seems you have turned a deaf ear,

I'm afraid I'll sink down in the depths,

afraid of the silence I hear.

When you answer I feel such great joy.

When you answer I dance and I sing.

I no longer need be afraid.

You protect me whatever life brings.

Psalm 29

The voice of the Lord

can feel like a storm,

crashing and whirling around.

Is this the voice of the Lord?

Are thunder and lightning,

terrible floods,

and earthquakes and fire

the voice of the Lord?

I'm afraid of such power,

destruction, and rage

in my life, in the world.

Is this the voice of the Lord?

Psalm 30

I was lost and you found me

deep in the pit of despair,

wailing and weeping at night,

with burdens too heavy to bear.

You brought me joy in the morning.

You're changing my mourning to dance,

removing the sackcloth and ashes.

Healing, you clothe me in gladness.

Psalm 31

Rejected and scorned,

in the gutter I land

like a jar that is broken,

discarded and damned.

But you are my fortress,

my strength and my shield,

protecting and loving.

To you I will yield.

Blessed be my God,

the one who now bears

all my troubles and burdens

and hears all my prayers.

Psalm 32

When I hide what I do

in sin and deceit,

soul and body are sick.

I can find no relief.

Like a mother with children,

God hears what I say.

When I tell her my sin,

all the pain goes away.

Psalm 33

Rejoice, oh you people of God,

and sing to the Lord a new song.

Make music with voices and strings!

Make music with cymbal and gong!

The earth overflows

with creation and love,

the waters below

and the heavens above.

Nations and kings

who think they are strong

and do not fear God

will prove to be wrong.

Blessed are they

who are humbled and awed,

who are hopeful and glad,

knowing love is God's law.

Psalm 34

(alphabetically)

Always be near me.

Be at my side.

Comfort and heal me.

Deeply I cry.

Evil departs as my

Fears are transformed.

God is redeeming and

Happiness born.

I bless the good Lord.

Join me in praise.

Kneeling in wonder,

Let us now pray.

Many our blessings,

No one's condemned.

Open our hearts.

Peace is within.

Quietly 'round us,

Radiant they stood

"Seek the Lord," said the angels,

"Taste and see all that's good."

Unbelief is now

Vanquished and victory

Won

Xylophones rippling that

Yahweh is blessing.

Zion is near us, and heaven's begun.

Psalm 35

Oh, God, I need your help,

for I am in despair.

Wake up, God, and hear my call,

for evil's in the air.

People gossip, telling lies,

and I am mocked and scorned.

They hate me without cause

when I have done no wrong.

When *they* were sick and needed help,

I fasted, prayed, and mourned,

yet now that I'm the one in need,

they laugh at me. I'm so forlorn.

God, fight my fights and strike them down

and trap them in their lies.

Then I will rejoice and say

how great you are, and wise.

Psalm 36

Some people would cheat

and others would steal

and think they can hide,

their sins not revealed.

But you are the judge,

and you judge us with love.

We're nestled by wings

of your spirit, the dove.

We feed at your table

and drink with delight.

May I never try hiding

my sins from your sight.

Psalm 37

Do not worry. Be at peace.

The wicked only seem to feast

and prosper in this time. Soon

God will make their evil cease.

Do not worry. Be at peace.

Jealousy brings no release.

Do good, and God alone will judge.

In God your riches will increase.

Psalm 38

I am sick and sore and weary.

Is there something I have done

to bring such misery and pain?

My friends have left. My foes have won.

I do not know what sin I did

to cause such illness in my core.

Be at my side. Forgive me, please.

I cannot live and suffer more.

Psalm 39

My mouth has sinned

with words and food,

spewing words out and stuffing food in.

With just one stroke

You have closed my mouth.

Words and food now make me choke.

Open my mouth

to bring you praise.

Gladden my heart

till the end of my days.

Psalm 40

When I was stuck,

you pulled me out.

When I was healed,

I could sing and shout

in praise of you

who brought me through.

No sacrifice did you require;

no offering did you desire.

How glad I am to sing your praise!

Be with me now for all my days.

Psalm 41

I'm sick again and in my bed.

My enemies now wish me dead,

and friends I trusted, rumors spread.

"He'll die in shame," is what they said.

Forgive me, God, for all my sins,

and make me healthy once again.

All praise to you. New life begins,

and I will laugh and play again.

Psalm 42

Why are you cast down, my soul,

and so disquieted with fear?

I feel forgotten, lost, alone.

But love and hope and help are near.

Psalm 43

Oh God, I go from faith to fear--

You seem so far away at times.

Send me light and truth again,

and then I'll sing you songs and rhymes.

Psalm 44

It used to be that we were strong,

but now we're scorned with words and deeds.

You've weakened us with death, disease,

when we've been faithful all along.

Psalm 45

Israel's king will wed today,

the oil of gladness on his head.

Blessed by God for all his deeds,

defending equity and truth,

he's giving hope to all in need.

His bride—his queen—is dressed in gold;

gold is woven in her robes.

A court of maidens leads the way

to the palace gates and enters in.

Her sons will rule the earth one day.

Psalm 46

God is our refuge and strength.

The waters may roar and the mountains shake,

but, "Be still and know I am God,"

for in God is our safety and faith.

Psalm 47

Sing to the Lord a new song.

Clap your hands and rejoice in a dance,

for victory reigns over all that is wrong,

and God gives us all a new chance.

Psalm 48

In the temple of God,

give praise and rejoice.

In city and mountain,

give praise and rejoice.

To the ends of the earth,

give praise and rejoice.

Tell all your children,

give praise and rejoice.

Psalm 49

Put no trust in your wealth –

rich and poor both will die.

Put your trust in your God,

for in God is your life.

.

Psalm 50

I am in the sunrise.

I am in the fire.

I see all the earth

and all good and bad desire.

Everything on earth is mine;

I made it with my hands.

I know every bird and beast

and creature in the lands.

I see who do the evil deeds,

who slander, lie and cheat,

then try to pacify my wrath

with offerings of meat.

Am I a hungry God

who'd eat the animals I made?

The only sacrifice I want

is thanksgiving and your praise.

Psalm 51

As the snowfall covers the ground

making everything new, white and clean,

create in me a clean heart.

Make my soul sparkle and gleam.

Fill me with joy and with gladness.

Cleanse me from all of my sins.

In contrition, I offer my prayer.

In thanksgiving, my new life begins.

Psalm 52

Violent rulers,

plotting destruction,

themselves become victims

of just retribution.

Rulers think riches

will be their protection,

but refuge in God

is the only salvation.

My trust is in God,

my love and devotion.

I can't be uprooted

by evil's destruction.

Psalm 53

Forced into exile, the people fled,

the enemy eating them like bread.

Wounded hearts and bodies bled.

"There is no God," the foolish said,

but God will strike the foolish dead.

Oh, bring deliverance, the people pray,

and we'll rejoice on that great day.

Psalm 54

I pray in your name.

My life's in your hand.

Save me from killers

who think they command.

Dear God, my helper,

for your saving arm

I praise you and thank you.

You've kept me from harm.

Psalm 55

The enemies without, I fight.

Betrayed by my familiar friend,

I have no strength to fight within.

He's been my equal in my sight.

We've worked and worshiped side by side,

but now his words have turned to lies.

His words, which sound so smooth and right,

have cut me like a pointed sword.

My broken heart I bring you, Lord.

Psalm 56

Dear God, you have kept my tears in a bottle,

my pleadings and prayers in a book.

Enemies surround me to trample me down,

but for safety to you I will look.

Psalm 57

Under your wings

I am safe in the storm.

No one can reach me

who wishes me harm.

They dug a deep pit

for me to fall in.

Instead they are trapped

by their own wicked sin.

Thank you, dear God.

I rejoice and I sing.

With you I can win!

Let drums and bells ring!

Psalm 58

The enemies who torture me

I want to torture back,

make them like the slimy snail

dissolving in its track,

or like water that dries up

and never will come back,

or like the grass, once green,

that shrivels and turns black.

Surely God agrees with me

and sanctions my attack.

Psalm 59

In the dark of the night

wild thoughts have been prowling

around in my mind,

menacing, growling.

What have I done?

I don't plot and scheme.

I've done nothing wrong.

My conscience is clean.

Where are these terrors

and snarling thoughts from?

Oh God, you must slay them.

Let no more fears come!

Psalm 60

Where is our God

when catastrophe strikes?

I want to lash out.

I want something to fight.

I want God on our side.

I want everything right.

I don't want to feel helpless,

or needy, or frightened.

Psalm 61

Protect me, oh God.

I long to feel safe,

and your strength is a rock

when I'm feeling so faint.

Protect me, oh God.

Hide me under your wing;

then praise and thanksgiving

are the songs I will sing.

Psalm 62

Power comes not from work I do

or whether I am rich or poor.

Power comes from God alone.

God is my rock, my refuge, my home.

Psalm 63

Seeking you, I thirst,

as if I'm in the desert sands.

Finding you, I burst

with joy. My life is in your hands.

Psalm 64

Hear my complaint:

they have no restraint

on their lies and their schemes

and words that blaspheme.

They ambush with traps

and hope I'll collapse.

They think they are hiding

when doing their spying,

but God sees them all.

Before God, they will fall,

and the righteous will glory

in telling this story.

Psalm 65

Joy is in the morning.

Hope is in the world.

You calm the storms of land and sea

and all the inner storms that swirl

within our hearts and minds,

forgiving us and blessing us.

You give us all we need,

and so in you we trust.

You bring rivers to the land,

and abundant growth of grain.

Pastures for the animals

you nourish with the rain.

Joy is in the morning.

Joy is in the day.

Joy is in the evening,

and joyfully I pray.

Psalm 66

Praise be to God,

who has seen us through trials

of water and fire.

Now reconciled,

we bring God our gifts,

and praise with our lips.

With no way through water,

he made ways on land.

With no way through fire,

he helped with his hand.

All you people, listen:

hear what God has done.

Our tests made us stronger.

Our troubles made us one.

Psalm 67

May God's face
shine upon us,
the face of love
still guide us.

And all of us
will praise her
for the harvest
from the earth.

Psalm 68

Let God arise in the morning clouds.

Let God arise in abundant rain.

Praise God who provides us the fruit and the grain.

The flocks have their meadows,

the homeless, a home.

God fathers the fatherless

and protects those alone.

Let the people arise in a joyful parade

with music and singing, with honor and praise,

bringing gifts back to God, who blesses our days.

Psalm 69

Dear God, I have sinned.

I thought I was right --

that the cause was for good,

that for you was my fight.

But now I am drowning

in all of my sin.

People hate and attack me.

I can't take it all in.

Please save me, oh God.

I am sinking in muck.

I'm up to my neck.

Oh, help me! I'm stuck.

Oh God, in your mercy,

forgive me and free me.

I will praise you forever.

Oh come! Intercede!

Psalm 70

Don't wait, oh my God,

or my fate will be death.

Make haste now to help me

before my last breath!

Let those who would kill me,

who say I'm to blame,

be brought to dishonor.

Let them feel the shame.

Hurry and help me,

now, in this hour!

Then I'll rejoice.

Great is your power.

Psalm 71

You were there when I was born.

When I was young, you taught me well.

My rock and fortress you became,

the place of safety where I dwell.

And now I'm old: my hair is gray,

my strength is gone. But you are strong.

I trust in you to keep me safe.

I'll sing your praises all day long.

Psalm 72

We pray for our country, oh God,

and blessings and health for our President,

who sees the oppressed and the needy,

and with wisdom and laws sets a precedent

to help the poor and the homeless.

We thank you for the man you have sent.

May peace and prosperity reign,

and abundance for all. We pray in God's name.

Psalm 73

It seems that the rich have it all—

sleek bodies, prosperity, pride,

praise as they walk down the street--

but their tongues strut the earth with their lies.

They wear their pride like a necklace.

Their bodies are covered with vice.

With malice, and hate, and oppression,

they get what they want out of life.

I almost fell into envy.

I've tried all my life to be good.

They do whatever they want, while

I've struggled to do what I should.

My strength is the strength of my God.

I asked God to help me in prayer.

I saw I have something they don't,

and nothing on earth can compare.

Their lives will end in their ruin,

while I have the riches that last.

For I have God's nearness and love,

but they think their fortune is cash.

Psalm 74

Our place of worship has been burned

and all our sacred vessels spurned.

Oh, God, how long

must this go on?

Why will you not strike them dead?

We had a covenant, you said.

Remember how you formed the seas?

You have the power. We pray you, please

to keep us safe and end this shame.

Our foes are taunting "God's to blame."

Psalm 75

Blessed be God's wonderful deeds.

He heard all our longings and pleas.

The wicked are brought to their knees.

The righteous will praise him indeed.

Psalm 76

Bring gifts to your God, who is Lord.

The oppressed of the earth have been saved!

Bring gifts of your vows and your deeds.

Bow down, all you mighty and brave,

for the Lord has broken the weapons of war,

and the terrible kings are no more.

Psalm 77

I'm awake in the night, and I worry.

I'm troubled and cry to my God.

My eyes will not close in the darkness.

My soul feels no comfort in God.

Then I think of God's wonders of old.

I remember his love and his power

when deep waters could not overwhelm me.

Then I'm comforted now, in *this* hour.

Psalm 78

Remember and tell all your children:

Remember the words of the Lord!

Remember and tell all your children:

Remember the works of the Lord.

He led you to safety from Egypt,

and when you were thirsty and dry,

He made water come out of the desert.

He answered your call and your cry.

Remember how much God provided!

How lavish the feast that you ate!

But you, as a people, forsook him,

rebelling, forgetting your faith.

So God gave your enemies strength

to punish the wicked and proud,

who worshipped the foreigner's gods.

Destruction and death he allowed.

But God has a heart of compassion

and forgave you, without killing all.

He raised up a Savior among you,

a shepherd, who answered his call.

Remember and tell all your children:

Remember the words of the Lord!

Remember and tell all your children:

Remember the works of the Lord!

Psalm 79

War and destruction

have laid us all low.

Jerusalem ruined,

we've no place to go.

Blood pours like water,

the bodies in piles.

Even the temple

our enemy defiles.

We are your people.

How long will this last?

Remember our worship!

Remember our past!

Pour out your anger

on our enemies' heads.

They mock us and scorn us.

Kill them instead!

Have compassion--forgive us!

Oh God, save us now.

We'll remember forever:

This is our vow.

Psalm 80

You brought us from Egypt,

held close in your hand,

and planted us safely

in this holy land.

We grew and we flourished

from rivers to seas,

our roots growing deep

and our branches like trees.

Now enemies strike us

and cut us all down.

They eat all our fruit,

and we're burned to the ground.

Oh, God, come to save us!

Let your face shine.

Give life once again

To your holy vine.

Psalm 81

I am your God.

I freed you from danger.

I lifted your burdens.

Do not worship strangers!

Don't harden your hearts--

listen only to me.

I'll fulfill all your longings

and give you a feast.

Now open your mouths.

I'll give all you can eat,

sweet honey from rocks

and the finest of wheat.

Psalm 82

Rescue the lost ones

who don't know what they seek.

They are walking in darkness,

needy and weak.

Psalm 83

Israel's surrounded.

Enemies hound us.

They are plotting in secret

to destroy and confound us.

Our future is dire.

Kill them with fire!

By your holy name,

put them to shame.

Psalm 84

How lovely is your dwelling place.

How lovely is this sacred space

where birds can nestle safe and sound

and sing their songs to all around,

where men and women enter in

to find the springs that nourish them.

A thousand others can't compare

to one day here in humble prayer.

Psalm 85

Remember the times that you saved us.

Remember the times you forgave us.

Look with favor again on our land

and send bountiful crops by your hand.

We'll listen again as you speak

and say love and righteousness meet.

When faithfulness springs from the ground,

then plenty and peace will abound.

Psalm 86

Help me and comfort me, Lord.

I ask you to come to my aid.

I know you are gracious and kind.

I'm in trouble and deeply afraid.

There are those who are seeking my life--

ruthless and insolent men.

I will praise you for all of my days,

if you save me, and life doesn't end.

Psalm 87

Glorious things are spoken of Zion,

for it is the city of God,

gathering all of God's people on earth

to make up the city of God.

Psalm 88

Despair and darkness surround me;

I'm forsaken as if in the grave.

I'm deep in the pit of depression,

and little remains to be saved.

Sick all my life since my childhood,

I pray every morning in bed.

You don't listen or answer my pleadings.

I'm helpless, destroyed, and near death.

Psalm 89

Lord, you have blessed David's line

and promised descendants forever.

But now enemies come to destroy us.

Strike down this evil endeavor!

Psalm 90

In all generations,

our home is in you.

We flourish and fade

Like the bright morning dew.

The days fly away

in the life of a man.

Bring wisdom each day

for the work of our hands.

Psalm 91

You who dwell in the shelter of God

are protected under her wings.

There nothing can hurt you or kill you,

no matter what enemies bring.

The angels watch over you always,

guarding you in all your ways.

Because you love your God dearly,

she will bless you for all your days.

Psalm 92

The person planted in God

 grows strong like the strongest tree,

bearing fruit even when old

as a sign for the world to see.

Sing praise to this wonderful God.

Make music with harp and with lyre.

Give thanks for the works of his hands

and the thoughts and the words he inspires.

Psalm 93

Oh Lord, you are mighty and strong.

Stronger than the waves of the sea,

stronger than the roaring of floods,

so strong are your holy decrees.

Psalm 94

You who are rulers,

your people are dying,

even innocent children.

And God hears their crying.

You are crushing your people

with bad statutes and debt,

with burdens too heavy,

and God won't forget.

You think God cannot hear?

You think God cannot see?

You can't escape judgment.

You have nowhere to flee.

Psalm 95

Sing to the Lord,

for he is gracious.

Sing to the Lord,

for he made us.

He made the dry land,

the mountains and seas.

Our world's in his hands.

Praise God on your knees.

God is our shepherd,

and we are his lambs.

He takes care of his flock.

We're safe in his hands.

Psalm 96

Sing to our God a new song,

for great is our God who has made us.

Through trials, temptations, and terrors,

give praise to the God who has saved us.

Heaven and earth shall sing to our God.

The oceans shall roar with their praise.

All crops in the fields and trees in the woods

Shall sing to our God all their days.

In beauty and strength lives our God,

majestic the works of his hands.

Honor and truth are his home.

Come worship the Lord, all you lands.

Psalm 97

God's judgments are glorious.

The whole earth rejoices.

The coastlands are singing.

The sky's filled with lightning.

Even mountains bow down.

The clouds are his throne.

Light comes at dawn as the darkness departs.

Those who give thanks will have joy in their hearts.

Psalm 98

Sing to our God a new song

for victory over all that's been wrong.

In melodious praise,

give thanks for these days

and make music to God all day long.

Psalm 99

Holy is our God,

the mighty, Holy One.

Holy is our God,

majestic on his throne.

Like a judge upon his throne,

he's fair and just to everyone.

Gather near and worship him!

Gratefully God's people come.

Psalm 100

Joyfully sing to our God,

gladly come near to our Lord,

happily serve him with song!

For he is the God who has made us

and, like children or sheep, protects us.

Give thanks for the ways he has blessed us.

God's love is enduring forever

for all countries and nations together

and to all generations forever.

Psalm 101

The king on his throne prays and speaks,

promising justice and peace.

Integrity rules in his heart;

malice and evil depart.

Those who slander and lie he'll destroy.

His household is filled now with joy.

The faithful will live in this land, and

the loyal will hear God's commands.

Psalm 102

The days pass like smoke,

and my bones are on fire.

I eat ashes with bread.

No tears quench this fire.

I wither like grass,

and my flesh melts away.

This life, like a garment,

will wear out and decay.

But you are eternal.

Your years have no end.

Generations to come

will praise you again.

Psalm 103

Bless the Lord, oh my soul!

Praise God from whom all blessings flow.

Bless God, you angels high above,

and all you creatures here below.

God redeemed me from the grave.

From ashes, now new life will grow.

I praise you, God, with heart and soul.

From God all love and mercy flow.

Psalm 104

All praise to God the great creator,

maker of the earth and sky;

clothed in light, the clouds your throne,

you ride the wings of wind and fly.

All praise to God the great creator

of oceans deep and mountains high,

of all the creatures great and small,

of birds and fish and butterflies.

All praise to God the great creator

of springs of water fresh and sweet,

of wine to make our hearts feel glad,

of plants and meat for all to eat.

Psalm 105

Remember our fathers and mothers.

Remember when we were enslaved.

Remember God brought us to freedom.

Remember how we have been saved.

Remember the God who is with us.

Remember the help that he brings.

Remember and tell all the people.

Remember, give praise now and sing.

Psalm 106

God freed us and made us a nation.

He took us away from oppression.

He led us in places uncharted,

but we couldn't be glad and wholehearted.

We looked back to what was familiar,

even the ways that were killing,

for new ways seemed hard and disturbing,

and the future far off and uncertain.

But God in his mercy forgave us,

and we, in thanksgiving, sing praises.

Psalm 107

God led us through the desert,

the dry places in our lives,

and satisfied our hungers.

He heard our thirsty cries.

God freed us from our prisons,

from the loads too much to bear,

from the broken, beaten places

and the depths of dark despair.

God saw our guilt and suffering

when we were dying from within.

When we asked for God's forgiveness,

we were healed of all our sin.

God heard us in the storms of life,

when we thought that we would die.

Instead, he brought us calmly home.

In arms of love, we safely lie.

Psalm 108

Sing to the mystery.

Sing to our history.

Sing to our victory!

Psalm 109

Some people curse and hate me,

even ones I love and pray for.

I've done nothing wrong against them.

Save me from this shame and war.

Let *their* evil deeds be punished,

they who've been so rich and greedy.

Let *their* children starve and suffer,

as they have the poor and needy.

In your mercy, come and save me—

take me from this dreadful place!

Let them know your love surrounds me.

Thank you, God. I rest my case.

Psalm 110

The Lord anoints you king,

and king and priest you'll be.

Other kings fall down before you

as you rule with equity.

Psalm 111

Alleluia! Sing praises to God

Because of his wonderful works.

Creation and comfort are the work of his hands.

Delight and trust are all he desires.

Everlasting his love,

Faithful his words,

Great are the works of his hands.

Psalm 112

Blessed are the ones who believe God and trust.

Blessed are the ones who are honest and just.

Blessed are the ones who share wealth with the poor.

Blessed are the faithful, steady and sure.

Psalm 113

Praise be to God

from sunrise to dusk,

for he raises us up

from ashes and dust

to sit in his kingdom,

to sit by his throne.

He gives women children.

He gives us a home.

Psalm 114

When the people fled Egypt,

God made the sea dry.

When the people were hungry,

manna fell from the sky.

The earth is the mother

even water obeyed

as it flowed from a rock,

so the people were saved.

Psalm 115

Don't worship a statue—

an object, a thing

with no heart to love you

and no arms to hug you.

No help will it bring.

Only God will give blessings,

only God, who is living.

It is God who is near us,

God who can hear us,

God alone who is giving.

Psalm 116

When I was sick and nearly dead,

I kept my faith, and what I said

was, "Save my life! I'm in distress!"

God heard my cry. My soul can rest.

I am your servant now, oh Lord,

you are the helper I adore.

This sacrifice of thanks and praise

is what I'll offer all my days.

Psalm 117

Let all the people praise you.

Let all the nations praise you

for your love for us together,

for your faithfulness forever.

Psalm 118

Enemies sought to destroy me,

but God is my rock and my light.

The stone that the builders rejected

became the support of my life.

God's love is enduring forever.

This is the day he has made.

Let us rejoice and be glad in it,

be strengthened and not be afraid.

Psalm 119

(alphabetically)

All God's laws are righteous and just.

Blessed are they who keep them.

Comfort me now in these troubled times.

Deal kindly with me when I fail.

Ever I seek to obey all your ways,

For my delight is to follow your laws.

Guide my feet in your pathways of truth.

Hold me fast in your love.

I am your servant in all that I do.

Judge me with mercy whenever I stray.

Keep your commandments down deep in my heart.

Let my lips always speak and sing praise.

Mornings I waken to study your laws.

Night times I worship and pray.

Open my heart to compassion and love.

Preserve my life to do your good works.

Quietly I ask you to save me.

Release me from those who oppress me.

Sweeter than honey are your words in my mouth.

Teach me the details of all of your laws, so

Understanding and knowledge are mine.

Virtue and honor I have sought all my days.

With all of my heart, I sing praises to you.

Examine my life that I've kept your decrees.

Your word is a lantern and light for my feet.

Zealously always I follow your light.

Psalm 120

I live in a land of liars and cheats

who don't listen to me when I speak.

They only want war, while I'm working for peace.

Psalm 121

I'm praying to God for some help

while I look at these beautiful hills.

God, who made heaven and earth,

says to be quiet and still.

God doesn't slumber or sleep.

She watches all day and all night

so I will not stumble or fall.

She protects me with all her great might.

Psalm 122

Pray for the peace of Jerusalem,

the beautiful city of God,

where all tribes and all nations come worship,

where I walked in the footsteps of God.

Psalm 123

The proud look down on the weak.

The rich look down on the poor.

I've had enough of contempt;

my eyes look up and see love.

Psalm 124

Had God looked away

when the enemy came,

we'd have died in a torrent

like floodwaters' rage.

But with God on our side

we escaped like a bird

flying safely away.

Our prayers had been heard.

Psalm 125

Those who trust in the Lord

are like mountains of stone

which can never be moved

to do anything wrong.

Psalm 126

In the time of our sorrow

we sowed only tears.

God brought us home laughing,

reaping bountiful years.

Psalm 127

Unless God builds your house,

you labor in vain.

Working early or late,

you have little to gain.

God does the work.

He doesn't slumber or sleep

but makes your life full

and at night gives you peace.

Psalm 128

Blessed are the people

who walk in God's ways:

fruitful your work

and happy your days.

Blessed are your children

and grandchildren too.

To God be the praise.

May peace be with you.

Psalm 129

When we formed our sacred nation,

enemies attacked and hurt us,

but God prevailed and turned them back.

Praise his name, for he preserved us.

Psalm 130

Out of the depths

I call on your name.

Listen to me!

I'm so full of shame.

Be merciful, please!

At the end of my rope,

I wait and I watch

for forgiveness and hope.

Psalm 131

Oh God, I feel humble and small,

like a child at her dear mother's breast.

I don't look for great things--

only calm for my soul, and some rest.

Psalm 132

Remember David's promise

to find the ark a home,

a special place for God to dwell

now Zion is his home.

The priests will bring salvation,

and the saints will shout for joy.

The hungry ones will all have bread,

and enemies will be destroyed.

Psalm 133

How good it is to be at peace,

in unity together.

It brings abundant blessings

overflowing on our heads

like rain upon a desert.

Psalm 134

Bless the Lord,

all priests and people,

and God will ever

bless and keep you.

Psalm 135

Praise God in the house of the Lord.

Praise God in the meadows and seas,

for he made all the heavens and earth,

and he made us and chose you and me.

He brought us through perils of death.

He freed us and saved all our lives.

Some turned to idols of gold,

but we follow God as our guide.

Psalm 136

Give thanks to the God of creation,

for his love is enduring forever.

Give thanks to the God who has made us,

for his love is enduring forever.

Give thanks to the God who has saved us,

for his love is enduring forever.

Psalm 137

We sat down and wept

when we were slaves in exile.

Our captors wanted dance and song

from us. They were so wrong.

How could we sing

with oppression in our mouths?

Revenge and hatred filled our hearts.

Oh God, destroy our captors now!

Psalm 138

All praise and thanks to you, oh God!

You answered me in my despair.

Your hand reached down and saved my life.

You touched the lowly with your care.

Fulfill your purpose in me now.

From love you made me with your hands.

In troubled times you kept me safe.

I kneel and wait for your commands.

Psalm 139

You knew me in the womb when I was being formed.

You knew me as a baby when I was newly born.

You know my thoughts and actions in everything
I do.

I go nowhere in the world that I'm not led by you.

How wonderful are all your works.

I bow to your life-giving words.

Psalm 140

Violent men are wanting war.

Words of poison spew from their lips.

May burning coals fall on their heads.

May they be thrown in yawning pits.

Let words of justice fill the air.

Praise to God who hears my prayer.

Psalm 141

I lift my voice in prayer, oh God,

the words like incense lifting up.

But guard my tongue and shut my lips

should any evil words erupt.

God keep me safe from evil ones.

How tempting are their dainty foods

when just one bite would be a trap.

May God catch *them* in traps they use.

Psalm 142

Oh God, I call for help from you.

I'm in a pit and can't get out.

My troubles overwhelm my soul.

No friends are near. I try to shout,

but no one hears or sees me here.

A black depression is my shroud.

This prison is too strong for me,

and only you can get me out.

Psalm 143

Hear my prayer and answer me!

My troubles crush me in a tomb.

My spirit faints. My soul is dry.

I thirst for you like desert blooms.

Hurry now and answer me!

And judge me not as I am due.

Teach me how to do your will.

I am your servant, trusting you.

Psalm 144

Oh God in your heavens,

who are we people

whom you care for and love

when our lives are so fleeting?

We reap a full harvest.

You give us daughters and sons.

We're blessed with abundance.

Happy our song.

Psalm 145

Our God is gracious and loving.

Our God is forgiving and kind.

Her mercy extends to all people.

She is happy with all she designed.

Our God lifts up those who are falling.

Our God holds us all in her hands.

She preserves all who worship and love her.

She rules justly in all of the lands.

In thanks we will praise her forever

and remember all she has done.

Generations will praise her forever,

for we'll teach all our daughters and sons.

Psalm 146

Do not worship earth's rulers

who change and die in their times.

Instead, put your trust in our God,

who is faithful, eternal, divine.

God cares for all his creation.

He opens the eyes of the blind.

He takes care of the widow and orphan.

To the stranger he's gracious and kind.

He opens the doors of the prisons

and gives justice to all the oppressed.

He gives plentiful food to the hungry

and lifts up those in distress.

Remember his reign is forever--

he created the earth and the skies.

Give praise to this God who has made us;

show honor and thanks with your lives.

Psalm 147

Give praise to our powerful God!

All who were exiled, rejoice!

for we have returned to our land.

Make music and lift up your voice!

Those who were broken in spirit

God touches to make their hearts whole.

Like water he brings to the desert,

he brings comfort and hope to our souls.

God makes the sunshine and rainfall.

God always cares for our needs.

He sends out his word to the fields

so our flocks and our crops will increase.

He blesses our families and children.

He makes peace on the borders with neighbors.

Sing praise to our powerful God.

Sing praise for his wonderful favors!

Psalm 148

Praise God for all he has made.

Praise God, all his heavenly host.

Praise God for the earth and the skies.

Praise God, all you people, rejoice!

Even the fish can sing praises,

the cattle and birds in the air,

the trees and the plants in the ground.

All people, praise God in your prayers!

Psalm 149

Sing to the Lord a new song.

Make music, sing praises, and dance.

God takes delight in his people,

and their enemies haven't a chance.

Psalm 150

Praise God in your houses of worship.

Praise him wherever you are.

Praise him because of his greatness.

Praise him, all the earth and the stars.

Praise him with trumpets and pipes.

Praise him with cymbals and harps.

Praise him with music and dance.

Praise him with all of your hearts.

www.ingramcontent.com/pod-product-compliance
Lightning Source LLC
Chambersburg PA
CBHW081254040426
42452CB00014B/2500